CHARMIDES

AND OTHER POEMS

By

OSCAR WILDE

First published in 1913

Read & Co.

Copyright © 2020 Ragged Hand

This edition is published by Ragged Hand,
an imprint of Read & Co.

This book is copyright and may not be reproduced or copied in any
way without the express permission of the publisher in writing.

British Library Cataloguing-in-Publication Data
A catalogue record for this book is available
from the British Library.

Read & Co. is part of Read Books Ltd.
For more information visit
www.readandcobooks.co.uk

CONTENTS

Oscar Wilde 5

POEMS

CHARMIDES. 7

REQUIESCAT 30

SAN MINIATO 31

ROME UNVISITED 32

HUMANITAD. 35

LOUIS NAPOLEON 50

ENDYMION (FOR MUSIC) 51

LE JARDIN. 53

LA MER. 54

LE PANNEAU 55

LES BALLONS. 57

CANZONET. 58

LE JARDIN DES TUILERIES 60

PAN DOUBLE VILLANELLE 61

IN THE FOREST. 63

SYMPHONY IN YELLOW 64

SONNETS

HÉLAS! 65

TO MILTON. 66

ON THE MASSACRE OF THE
CHRISTIANS IN BULGARIA 67

HOLY WEEK AT GENOA. 68

URBS SACRA ÆTERNA 69

E TENEBRIS. 70

AT VERONA 71

ON THE SALE BY AUCTION OF KEATS'
LOVE LETTERS 72

THE NEW REMORSE 73

OSCAR WILDE

Oscar Fingal O'Flahertie Wills Wilde was born in Dublin in 1854. His parents were successful Dublin intellectuals, and Wilde became fluent in French and German early in life. He studied at Trinity College, Dublin, and subsequently won a scholarship to Magdalen College, Oxford, where he was heavily influenced by John Ruskin and Walter Pate. Wilde proved himself to be an outstanding classicist. After university, he moved to London and became involved with the fashionable cultural and social circles of the day. At the age of just 25 he was well-known as a wit and a dandy, and as a spokesman for aestheticism—an artistic movement that emphasized aesthetic values ahead of socio-political themes—he undertook a lecture tour to the United States in 1882, before eventually returning to London to try his hand at journalism. It was also around this time that he produced most of his well-known short fiction.

In 1891, Wilde published *The Picture of Dorian Gray,* his only novel. Reviewers criticised the novel's decadence and homosexual allusions, although it was popular nonetheless. From 1892, Wilde focussed on playwriting. In that year, he gained commercial and critical success with *Lady Windermere's Fan,* and followed it with the comedy *A Woman of No Importance* (1893) and *An Ideal Husband* (1895). Then came Wilde's most famous play, *The Importance of Being Earnest* – a farcical comedy which cemented his artistic reputation and is now seen as his masterpiece.

In 1895, the Marquess of Queensbury, who objected to his son spending so much time with Wilde because of Wilde's flamboyant behaviour and reputation, publicly insulted him. In response, Wilde brought an unsuccessful slander suit against him. The result of this inability to prove slander was his own trial on charges of sodomy, and the revealing to the transfixed Victorian public of salacious details of Wilde's private life followed. Wilde was found guilty and sentenced to two years of hard labour.

Wilde was released from prison in 1897, having suffered from a number of ailments and injuries. He left England the next day for the continent, to spend his last three years in penniless exile. He settled in Paris, and didn't write anymore, declaring "I can write, but have lost the joy of writing." Wilde died of cerebral meningitis on in November of 1900, converting to Catholicism on his deathbed.

POEMS

CHARMIDES

——————————

I

He was a Grecian lad, who coming home
    With pulpy figs and wine from Sicily
Stood at his galley's prow, and let the foam
    Blow through his crisp brown curls unconsciously,
And holding wave and wind in boy's despite
Peered from his dripping seat across the wet and stormy night.

Till with the dawn he saw a burnished spear
    Like a thin thread of gold against the sky,
And hoisted sail, and strained the creaking gear,
    And bade the pilot head her lustily
Against the nor'west gale, and all day long
Held on his way, and marked the rowers' time with measured song.

And when the faint Corinthian hills were red
    Dropped anchor in a little sandy bay,
And with fresh boughs of olive crowned his head,
    And brushed from cheek and throat the hoary spray,
And washed his limbs with oil, and from the hold
Brought out his linen tunic and his sandals brazen-soled,

And a rich robe stained with the fishers' juice
    Which of some swarthy trader he had bought
Upon the sunny quay at Syracuse,
    And was with Tyrian broideries inwrought,
And by the questioning merchants made his way
Up through the soft and silver woods, and when the labouring day

Had spun its tangled web of crimson cloud,
    Clomb the high hill, and with swift silent feet
Crept to the fane unnoticed by the crowd
    Of busy priests, and from some dark retreat
Watched the young swains his frolic playmates bring
The firstling of their little flock, and the shy shepherd fling

The crackling salt upon the flame, or hang
    His studded crook against the temple wall
To Her who keeps away the ravenous fang
    Of the base wolf from homestead and from stall;
And then the clear-voiced maidens 'gan to sing,
And to the altar each man brought some goodly offering,

A beechen cup brimming with milky foam,
    A fair cloth wrought with cunning imagery
Of hounds in chase, a waxen honey-comb
    Dripping with oozy gold which scarce the bee
Had ceased from building, a black skin of oil
Meet for the wrestlers, a great boar the fierce and white-tusked spoil

Stolen from Artemis that jealous maid
    To please Athena, and the dappled hide
Of a tall stag who in some mountain glade
    Had met the shaft; and then the herald cried,
And from the pillared precinct one by one
Went the glad Greeks well pleased that they their simple vows had done.

And the old priest put out the waning fires
    Save that one lamp whose restless ruby glowed
For ever in the cell, and the shrill lyres
    Came fainter on the wind, as down the road
In joyous dance these country folk did pass,
And with stout hands the warder closed the gates of polished brass.

Long time he lay and hardly dared to breathe,
    And heard the cadenced drip of spilt-out wine,
And the rose-petals falling from the wreath
    As the night breezes wandered through the shrine,
And seemed to be in some entrancèd swoon
Till through the open roof above the full and brimming moon

Flooded with sheeny waves the marble floor,
    When from his nook up leapt the venturous lad,
And flinging wide the cedar-carven door
    Beheld an awful image saffron-clad
And armed for battle! the gaunt Griffin glared
From the huge helm, and the long lance of wreck and ruin flared

Like a red rod of flame, stony and steeled
    The Gorgon's head its leaden eyeballs rolled,
And writhed its snaky horrors through the shield,
    And gaped aghast with bloodless lips and cold
In passion impotent, while with blind gaze
The blinking owl between the feet hooted in shrill amaze.

The lonely fisher as he trimmed his lamp
    Far out at sea off Sunium, or cast
The net for tunnies, heard a brazen tramp
    Of horses smite the waves, and a wild blast
Divide the folded curtains of the night,
And knelt upon the little poop, and prayed in holy fright.

And guilty lovers in their venery
    Forgat a little while their stolen sweets,
Deeming they heard dread Dian's bitter cry;
    And the grim watchmen on their lofty seats
Ran to their shields in haste precipitate,
Or strained black-bearded throats across the dusky parapet.

For round the temple rolled the clang of arms,
    And the twelve Gods leapt up in marble fear,
And the air quaked with dissonant alarums
    Till huge Poseidon shook his mighty spear,
And on the frieze the prancing horses neighed,
And the low tread of hurrying feet rang from the cavalcade.

Ready for death with parted lips he stood,
    And well content at such a price to see
That calm wide brow, that terrible maidenhood,
    The marvel of that pitiless chastity,
Ah! well content indeed, for never wight
Since Troy's young shepherd prince had seen so wonderful a sight.

Ready for death he stood, but lo! the air
    Grew silent, and the horses ceased to neigh,
And off his brow he tossed the clustering hair,
    And from his limbs he throw the cloak away;
For whom would not such love make desperate?
And nigher came, and touched her throat, and with hands violate

Undid the cuirass, and the crocus gown,
    And bared the breasts of polished ivory,
Till from the waist the peplos falling down
    Left visible the secret mystery
Which to no lover will Athena show,
The grand cool flanks, the crescent thighs, the bossy hills of snow.

Those who have never known a lover's sin
    Let them not read my ditty, it will be
To their dull ears so musicless and thin
    That they will have no joy of it, but ye
To whose wan cheeks now creeps the lingering smile,
Ye who have learned who Eros is,—O listen yet awhile.

A little space he let his greedy eyes
    Rest on the burnished image, till mere sight
Half swooned for surfeit of such luxuries,
    And then his lips in hungering delight
Fed on her lips, and round the towered neck
He flung his arms, nor cared at all his passion's will to check.

Never I ween did lover hold such tryst,
    For all night long he murmured honeyed word,
And saw her sweet unravished limbs, and kissed
    Her pale and argent body undisturbed,
And paddled with the polished throat, and pressed
His hot and beating heart upon her chill and icy breast.

It was as if Numidian javelins
    Pierced through and through his wild and whirling brain,
And his nerves thrilled like throbbing violins
    In exquisite pulsation, and the pain
Was such sweet anguish that he never drew
His lips from hers till overhead the lark of warning flew.

They who have never seen the daylight peer
    Into a darkened room, and drawn the curtain,
And with dull eyes and wearied from some dear
    And worshipped body risen, they for certain
Will never know of what I try to sing,
How long the last kiss was, how fond and late his lingering.

11

The moon was girdled with a crystal rim,
   The sign which shipmen say is ominous
Of wrath in heaven, the wan stars were dim,
   And the low lightening east was tremulous
With the faint fluttering wings of flying dawn,
Ere from the silent sombre shrine his lover had withdrawn.

Down the steep rock with hurried feet and fast
   Clomb the brave lad, and reached the cave of Pan,
And heard the goat-foot snoring as he passed,
   And leapt upon a grassy knoll and ran
Like a young fawn unto an olive wood
Which in a shady valley by the well-built city stood;

And sought a little stream, which well he knew,
   For oftentimes with boyish careless shout
The green and crested grebe he would pursue,
   Or snare in woven net the silver trout,
And down amid the startled reeds he lay
Panting in breathless sweet affright, and waited for the day.

On the green bank he lay, and let one hand
   Dip in the cool dark eddies listlessly,
And soon the breath of morning came and fanned
   His hot flushed cheeks, or lifted wantonly
The tangled curls from off his forehead, while
He on the running water gazed with strange and secret smile.

And soon the shepherd in rough woollen cloak
   With his long crook undid the wattled cotes,
And from the stack a thin blue wreath of smoke
   Curled through the air across the ripening oats,
And on the hill the yellow house-dog bayed
As through the crisp and rustling fern the heavy cattle strayed.

And when the light-foot mower went afield
    Across the meadows laced with threaded dew,
And the sheep bleated on the misty weald,
    And from its nest the waking corncrake flew,
Some woodmen saw him lying by the stream
And marvelled much that any lad so beautiful could seem,

Nor deemed him born of mortals, and one said,
    'It is young Hylas, that false runaway
Who with a Naiad now would make his bed
    Forgetting Herakles,' but others, 'Nay,
It is Narcissus, his own paramour,
Those are the fond and crimson lips no woman can allure.'

And when they nearer came a third one cried,
    'It is young Dionysos who has hid
His spear and fawnskin by the river side
    Weary of hunting with the Bassarid,
And wise indeed were we away to fly:
They live not long who on the gods immortal come to spy.'

So turned they back, and feared to look behind,
    And told the timid swain how they had seen
Amid the reeds some woodland god reclined,
    And no man dared to cross the open green,
And on that day no olive-tree was slain,
Nor rushes cut, but all deserted was the fair domain,

Save when the neat-herd's lad, his empty pail
    Well slung upon his back, with leap and bound
Raced on the other side, and stopped to hail,
    Hoping that he some comrade new had found,
And gat no answer, and then half afraid
Passed on his simple way, or down the still and silent glade

A little girl ran laughing from the farm,
   Not thinking of love's secret mysteries,
And when she saw the white and gleaming arm
   And all his manlihood, with longing eyes
Whose passion mocked her sweet virginity
Watched him awhile, and then stole back sadly and wearily.

Far off he heard the city's hum and noise,
   And now and then the shriller laughter where
The passionate purity of brown-limbed boys
   Wrestled or raced in the clear healthful air,
And now and then a little tinkling bell
As the shorn wether led the sheep down to the mossy well.

Through the grey willows danced the fretful gnat,
   The grasshopper chirped idly from the tree,
In sleek and oily coat the water-rat
   Breasting the little ripples manfully
Made for the wild-duck's nest, from bough to bough
Hopped the shy finch, and the huge tortoise crept across the slough.

On the faint wind floated the silky seeds
   As the bright scythe swept through the waving grass,
The ouzel-cock splashed circles in the reeds
   And flecked with silver whorls the forest's glass,
Which scarce had caught again its imagery
Ere from its bed the dusky tench leapt at the dragon-fly.

But little care had he for any thing
   Though up and down the beech the squirrel played,
And from the copse the linnet 'gan to sing
   To its brown mate its sweetest serenade;
Ah! little care indeed, for he had seen
The breasts of Pallas and the naked wonder of the Queen.

But when the herdsman called his straggling goats
    With whistling pipe across the rocky road,
And the shard-beetle with its trumpet-notes
    Boomed through the darkening woods, and seemed to bode
Of coming storm, and the belated crane
Passed homeward like a shadow, and the dull big drops of rain

Fell on the pattering fig-leaves, up he rose,
    And from the gloomy forest went his way
Past sombre homestead and wet orchard-close,
    And came at last unto a little quay,
And called his mates aboard, and took his seat
On the high poop, and pushed from land, and loosed the dripping sheet,

And steered across the bay, and when nine suns
    Passed down the long and laddered way of gold,
And nine pale moons had breathed their orisons
    To the chaste stars their confessors, or told
Their dearest secret to the downy moth
That will not fly at noonday, through the foam and surging froth

Came a great owl with yellow sulphurous eyes
    And lit upon the ship, whose timbers creaked
As though the lading of three argosies
    Were in the hold, and flapped its wings and shrieked,
And darkness straightway stole across the deep,
Sheathed was Orion's sword, dread Mars himself fled down the steep,

And the moon hid behind a tawny mask
    Of drifting cloud, and from the ocean's marge
Rose the red plume, the huge and hornèd casque,
    The seven-cubit spear, the brazen targe!
And clad in bright and burnished panoply
Athena strode across the stretch of sick and shivering sea!

To the dull sailors' sight her loosened looks
    Seemed like the jagged storm-rack, and her feet
Only the spume that floats on hidden rocks,
    And, marking how the rising waters beat
Against the rolling ship, the pilot cried
To the young helmsman at the stern to luff to windward side

But he, the overbold adulterer,
    A dear profaner of great mysteries,
An ardent amorous idolater,
    When he beheld those grand relentless eyes
Laughed loud for joy, and crying out 'I come'
Leapt from the lofty poop into the chill and churning foam.

Then fell from the high heaven one bright star,
    One dancer left the circling galaxy,
And back to Athens on her clattering car
    In all the pride of venged divinity
Pale Pallas swept with shrill and steely clank,
And a few gurgling bubbles rose where her boy lover sank.

And the mast shuddered as the gaunt owl flew
    With mocking hoots after the wrathful Queen,
And the old pilot bade the trembling crew
    Hoist the big sail, and told how he had seen
Close to the stern a dim and giant form,
And like a dipping swallow the stout ship dashed through the storm.

And no man dared to speak of Charmides
    Deeming that he some evil thing had wrought,
And when they reached the strait Symplegades
    They beached their galley on the shore, and sought
The toll-gate of the city hastily,
And in the market showed their brown and pictured pottery.

II

But some good Triton-god had ruth, and bare
    The boy's drowned body back to Grecian land,
And mermaids combed his dank and dripping hair
    And smoothed his brow, and loosed his clenching hand;
Some brought sweet spices from far Araby,
And others bade the halcyon sing her softest lullaby.

And when he neared his old Athenian home,
    A mighty billow rose up suddenly
Upon whose oily back the clotted foam
    Lay diapered in some strange fantasy,
And clasping him unto its glassy breast
Swept landward, like a white-maned steed upon a venturous quest!

Now where Colonos leans unto the sea
    There lies a long and level stretch of lawn;
The rabbit knows it, and the mountain bee
    For it deserts Hymettus, and the Faun
Is not afraid, for never through the day
Comes a cry ruder than the shout of shepherd lads at play.

But often from the thorny labyrinth
    And tangled branches of the circling wood
The stealthy hunter sees young Hyacinth
    Hurling the polished disk, and draws his hood
Over his guilty gaze, and creeps away,
Nor dares to wind his horn, or—else at the first break of day

The Dryads come and throw the leathern ball
    Along the reedy shore, and circumvent
Some goat-eared Pan to be their seneschal
    For fear of bold Poseidon's ravishment,
And loose their girdles, with shy timorous eyes,
Lest from the surf his azure arms and purple beard should rise.

On this side and on that a rocky cave,
    Hung with the yellow-belled laburnum, stands
Smooth is the beach, save where some ebbing wave
    Leaves its faint outline etched upon the sands,
As though it feared to be too soon forgot
By the green rush, its playfellow,—and yet, it is a spot

So small, that the inconstant butterfly
    Could steal the hoarded money from each flower
Ere it was noon, and still not satisfy
    Its over-greedy love,—within an hour
A sailor boy, were he but rude enow
To land and pluck a garland for his galley's painted prow,

Would almost leave the little meadow bare,
    For it knows nothing of great pageantry,
Only a few narcissi here and there
    Stand separate in sweet austerity,
Dotting the unmown grass with silver stars,
And here and there a daffodil waves tiny scimitars.

Hither the billow brought him, and was glad
    Of such dear servitude, and where the land
Was virgin of all waters laid the lad
    Upon the golden margent of the strand,
And like a lingering lover oft returned
To kiss those pallid limbs which once with intense fire burned,

Ere the wet seas had quenched that holocaust,
    That self-fed flame, that passionate lustihead,
Ere grisly death with chill and nipping frost
    Had withered up those lilies white and red
Which, while the boy would through the forest range,
Answered each other in a sweet antiphonal counter-change.

And when at dawn the wood-nymphs, hand-in-hand,
    Threaded the bosky dell, their satyr spied
The boy's pale body stretched upon the sand,
    And feared Poseidon's treachery, and cried,
And like bright sunbeams flitting through a glade
Each startled Dryad sought some safe and leafy ambuscade.

Save one white girl, who deemed it would not be
    So dread a thing to feel a sea-god's arms
Crushing her breasts in amorous tyranny,
    And longed to listen to those subtle charms
Insidious lovers weave when they would win
Some fencèd fortress, and stole back again, nor thought it sin

To yield her treasure unto one so fair,
    And lay beside him, thirsty with love's drouth,
Called him soft names, played with his tangled hair,
    And with hot lips made havoc of his mouth
Afraid he might not wake, and then afraid
Lest he might wake too soon, fled back, and then, fond renegade,

Returned to fresh assault, and all day long
    Sat at his side, and laughed at her new toy,
And held his hand, and sang her sweetest song,
    Then frowned to see how froward was the boy
Who would not with her maidenhood entwine,
Nor knew that three days since his eyes had looked on Proserpine;

19

Nor knew what sacrilege his lips had done,
    But said, 'He will awake, I know him well,
He will awake at evening when the sun
    Hangs his red shield on Corinth's citadel;
This sleep is but a cruel treachery
To make me love him more, and in some cavern of the sea

Deeper than ever falls the fisher's line
    Already a huge Triton blows his horn,
And weaves a garland from the crystalline
    And drifting ocean-tendrils to adorn
The emerald pillars of our bridal bed,
For sphered in foaming silver, and with coral crownèd head,

We two will sit upon a throne of pearl,
    And a blue wave will be our canopy,
And at our feet the water-snakes will curl
    In all their amethystine panoply
Of diamonded mail, and we will mark
The mullets swimming by the mast of some storm-foundered bark,

Vermilion-finned with eyes of bossy gold
    Like flakes of crimson light, and the great deep
His glassy-portaled chamber will unfold,
    And we will see the painted dolphins sleep
Cradled by murmuring halcyons on the rocks
Where Proteus in quaint suit of green pastures his monstrous flocks.

And tremulous opal-hued anemones
    Will wave their purple fringes where we tread
Upon the mirrored floor, and argosies
    Of fishes flecked with tawny scales will thread
The drifting cordage of the shattered wreck,
And honey-coloured amber beads our twining limbs will deck.'

But when that baffled Lord of War the Sun
　　With gaudy pennon flying passed away
Into his brazen House, and one by one
　　The little yellow stars began to stray
Across the field of heaven, ah! then indeed
She feared his lips upon her lips would never care to feed,

And cried, 'Awake, already the pale moon
　　Washes the trees with silver, and the wave
Creeps grey and chilly up this sandy dune,
　　The croaking frogs are out, and from the cave
The nightjar shrieks, the fluttering bats repass,
And the brown stoat with hollow flanks creeps through the dusky grass.

Nay, though thou art a god, be not so coy,
　　For in yon stream there is a little reed
That often whispers how a lovely boy
　　Lay with her once upon a grassy mead,
Who when his cruel pleasure he had done
Spread wings of rustling gold and soared aloft into the sun.

Be not so coy, the laurel trembles still
　　With great Apollo's kisses, and the fir
Whose clustering sisters fringe the seaward hill
　　Hath many a tale of that bold ravisher
Whom men call Boreas, and I have seen
The mocking eyes of Hermes through the poplar's silvery sheen.

Even the jealous Naiads call me fair,
　　And every morn a young and ruddy swain
Woos me with apples and with locks of hair,
　　And seeks to soothe my virginal disdain
By all the gifts the gentle wood-nymphs love;
But yesterday he brought to me an iris-plumaged dove

With little crimson feet, which with its store
    Of seven spotted eggs the cruel lad
Had stolen from the lofty sycamore
    At daybreak, when her amorous comrade had
Flown off in search of berried juniper
Which most they love; the fretful wasp, that earliest vintager

Of the blue grapes, hath not persistency
    So constant as this simple shepherd-boy
For my poor lips, his joyous purity
    And laughing sunny eyes might well decoy
A Dryad from her oath to Artemis;
For very beautiful is he, his mouth was made to kiss;

His argent forehead, like a rising moon
    Over the dusky hills of meeting brows,
Is crescent shaped, the hot and Tyrian noon
    Leads from the myrtle-grove no goodlier spouse
For Cytheræa, the first silky down
Fringes his blushing cheeks, and his young limbs are strong and brown;

And he is rich, and fat and fleecy herds
    Of bleating sheep upon his meadows lie,
And many an earthen bowl of yellow curds
    Is in his homestead for the thievish fly
To swim and drown in, the pink clover mead
Keeps its sweet store for him, and he can pipe on oaten reed.

And yet I love him not; it was for thee
    I kept my love; I knew that thou would'st come
To rid me of this pallid chastity,
    Thou fairest flower of the flowerless foam
Of all the wide Ægean, brightest star
Of ocean's azure heavens where the mirrored planets are!

I knew that thou would'st come, for when at first
    The dry wood burgeoned, and the sap of spring
Swelled in my green and tender bark or burst
    To myriad multitudinous blossoming
Which mocked the midnight with its mimic moons
That did not dread the dawn, and first the thrushes' rapturous tunes

Startled the squirrel from its granary,
    And cuckoo flowers fringed the narrow lane,
Through my young leaves a sensuous ecstasy
    Crept like new wine, and every mossy vein
Throbbed with the fitful pulse of amorous blood,
And the wild winds of passion shook my slim stem's maidenhood.

The trooping fawns at evening came and laid
    Their cool black noses on my lowest boughs,
And on my topmost branch the blackbird made
    A little nest of grasses for his spouse,
And now and then a twittering wren would light
On a thin twig which hardly bare the weight of such delight.

I was the Attic shepherd's trysting place,
    Beneath my shadow Amaryllis lay,
And round my trunk would laughing Daphnis chase
    The timorous girl, till tired out with play
She felt his hot breath stir her tangled hair,
And turned, and looked, and fled no more from such delightful snare.

Then come away unto my ambuscade
    Where clustering woodbine weaves a canopy
For amorous pleasaunce, and the rustling shade
    Of Paphian myrtles seems to sanctify
The dearest rites of love; there in the cool
And green recesses of its farthest depth there is pool,

The ouzel's haunt, the wild bee's pasturage,
　　For round its rim great creamy lilies float
Through their flat leaves in verdant anchorage,
　　Each cup a white-sailed golden-laden boat
Steered by a dragon-fly,—be not afraid
To leave this wan and wave-kissed shore, surely the place was made

For lovers such as we; the Cyprian Queen,
　　One arm around her boyish paramour,
Strays often there at eve, and I have seen
　　The moon strip off her misty vestiture
For young Endymion's eyes; be not afraid,
The panther feet of Dian never tread that secret glade.

Nay if thou will'st, back to the beating brine,
　　Back to the boisterous billow let us go,
And walk all day beneath the hyaline
　　Huge vault of Neptune's watery portico,
And watch the purple monsters of the deep
Sport in ungainly play, and from his lair keen Xiphias leap.

For if my mistress find me lying here
　　She will not ruth or gentle pity show,
But lay her boar-spear down, and with austere
　　Relentless fingers string the cornel bow,
And draw the feathered notch against her breast,
And loose the archèd cord; aye, even now upon the quest

I hear her hurrying feet,—awake, awake,
　　Thou laggard in love's battle! once at least
Let me drink deep of passion's wine, and slake
　　My parchèd being with the nectarous feast
Which even gods affect! O come, Love, come,
Still we have time to reach the cavern of thine azure home.'

Scarce had she spoken when the shuddering trees
    Shook, and the leaves divided, and the air
Grew conscious of a god, and the grey seas
    Crawled backward, and a long and dismal blare
Blew from some tasselled horn, a sleuth-hound bayed,
And like a flame a barbèd reed flew whizzing down the glade.

And where the little flowers of her breast
    Just brake into their milky blossoming,
This murderous paramour, this unbidden guest,
    Pierced and struck deep in horrid chambering,
And ploughed a bloody furrow with its dart,
And dug a long red road, and cleft with wingèd death her heart.

Sobbing her life out with a bitter cry
    On the boy's body fell the Dryad maid,
Sobbing for incomplete virginity,
    And raptures unenjoyed, and pleasures dead,
And all the pain of things unsatisfied,
And the bright drops of crimson youth crept down her throbbing side.

Ah! pitiful it was to hear her moan,
    And very pitiful to see her die
Ere she had yielded up her sweets, or known
    The joy of passion, that dread mystery
Which not to know is not to live at all,
And yet to know is to be held in death's most deadly thrall.

But as it hapt the Queen of Cythere,
    Who with Adonis all night long had lain
Within some shepherd's hut in Arcady,
    On team of silver doves and gilded wain
Was journeying Paphos-ward, high up afar
From mortal ken between the mountains and the morning star,

And when low down she spied the hapless pair,
    And heard the Oread's faint despairing cry,
Whose cadence seemed to play upon the air
    As though it were a viol, hastily
She bade her pigeons fold each straining plume,
And dropt to earth, and reached the strand, and saw their dolorous doom.

For as a gardener turning back his head
    To catch the last notes of the linnet, mows
With careless scythe too near some flower bed,
    And cuts the thorny pillar of the rose,
And with the flower's loosened loneliness
Strews the brown mould; or as some shepherd lad in wantonness

Driving his little flock along the mead
    Treads down two daffodils, which side by aide
Have lured the lady-bird with yellow brede
    And made the gaudy moth forget its pride,
Treads down their brimming golden chalices
Under light feet which were not made for such rude ravages;

Or as a schoolboy tired of his book
    Flings himself down upon the reedy grass
And plucks two water-lilies from the brook,
    And for a time forgets the hour glass,
Then wearies of their sweets, and goes his way,
And lets the hot sun kill them, even go these lovers lay.

And Venus cried, 'It is dread Artemis
    Whose bitter hand hath wrought this cruelty,
Or else that mightier maid whose care it is
    To guard her strong and stainless majesty
Upon the hill Athenian,—alas!
That they who loved so well unloved into Death's house should pass.'

So with soft hands she laid the boy and girl
   In the great golden waggon tenderly
(Her white throat whiter than a moony pearl
   Just threaded with a blue vein's tapestry
Had not yet ceased to throb, and still her breast
Swayed like a wind-stirred lily in ambiguous unrest)

And then each pigeon spread its milky van,
   The bright car soared into the dawning sky,
And like a cloud the aerial caravan
   Passed over the Ægean silently,
Till the faint air was troubled with the song
From the wan mouths that call on bleeding Thammuz all night long.

But when the doves had reached their wonted goal
   Where the wide stair of orbèd marble dips
Its snows into the sea, her fluttering soul
   Just shook the trembling petals of her lips
And passed into the void, and Venus knew
That one fair maid the less would walk amid her retinue,

And bade her servants carve a cedar chest
   With all the wonder of this history,
Within whose scented womb their limbs should rest
   Where olive-trees make tender the blue sky
On the low hills of Paphos, and the Faun
Pipes in the noonday, and the nightingale sings on till dawn.

Nor failed they to obey her hest, and ere
   The morning bee had stung the daffodil
With tiny fretful spear, or from its lair
   The waking stag had leapt across the rill
And roused the ouzel, or the lizard crept
Athwart the sunny rock, beneath the grass their bodies slept.

And when day brake, within that silver shrine
   Fed by the flames of cressets tremulous,
Queen Venus knelt and prayed to Proserpine
   That she whose beauty made Death amorous
Should beg a guerdon from her pallid Lord,
And let Desire pass across dread Charon's icy ford.

III

In melancholy moonless Acheron,
   Farm for the goodly earth and joyous day
Where no spring ever buds, nor ripening sun
   Weighs down the apple trees, nor flowery May
Chequers with chestnut blooms the grassy floor,
Where thrushes never sing, and piping linnets mate no more,

There by a dim and dark Lethæan well
   Young Charmides was lying; wearily
He plucked the blossoms from the asphodel,
   And with its little rifled treasury
Strewed the dull waters of the dusky stream,
And watched the white stars founder, and the land was like a dream,

When as he gazed into the watery glass
   And through his brown hair's curly tangles scanned
His own wan face, a shadow seemed to pass
   Across the mirror, and a little hand
Stole into his, and warm lips timidly
Brushed his pale cheeks, and breathed their secret forth into a sigh.

Then turned he round his weary eyes and saw,
    And ever nigher still their faces came,
And nigher ever did their young mouths draw
    Until they seemed one perfect rose of flame,
And longing arms around her neck he cast,
And felt her throbbing bosom, and his breath came hot and fast,

And all his hoarded sweets were hers to kiss,
    And all her maidenhood was his to slay,
And limb to limb in long and rapturous bliss
    Their passion waxed and waned,—O why essay
To pipe again of love, too venturous reed!
Enough, enough that Eros laughed upon that flowerless mead.

Too venturous poesy, O why essay
    To pipe again of passion! fold thy wings
O'er daring Icarus and bid thy lay
    Sleep hidden in the lyre's silent strings
Till thou hast found the old Castalian rill,
Or from the Lesbian waters plucked drowned Sappho's golden quid!

Enough, enough that he whose life had been
    A fiery pulse of sin, a splendid shame,
Could in the loveless land of Hades glean
    One scorching harvest from those fields of flame
Where passion walks with naked unshod feet
And is not wounded,—ah! enough that once their lips could meet

In that wild throb when all existences
    Seemed narrowed to one single ecstasy
Which dies through its own sweetness and the stress
    Of too much pleasure, ere Persephone
Had bade them serve her by the ebon throne
Of the pale God who in the fields of Enna loosed her zone.

29

REQUIESCAT

Tread lightly, she is near
    Under the snow,
Speak gently, she can hear
    The daisies grow.

All her bright golden hair
    Tarnished with rust,
She that was young and fair
    Fallen to dust.

Lily-like, white as snow,
    She hardly knew
She was a woman, so
    Sweetly she grew.

Coffin-board, heavy stone,
    Lie on her breast,
I vex my heart alone,
    She is at rest.

Peace, Peace, she cannot hear
    Lyre or sonnet,
All my life's buried here,
    Heap earth upon it.

AVIGNON

SAN MINIATO

See, I have climbed the mountain side
   Up to this holy house of God,
   Where once that Angel-Painter trod
Who saw the heavens opened wide,

And throned upon the crescent moon
   The Virginal white Queen of Grace,—
   Mary! could I but see thy face
Death could not come at all too soon.

O crowned by God with thorns and pain!
   Mother of Christ! O mystic wife!
   My heart is weary of this life
And over-sad to sing again.

O crowned by God with love and flame!
   O crowned by Christ the Holy One!
   O listen ere the searching sun
Show to the world my sin and shame.

ROME UNVISITED

I

The corn has turned from grey to red,
  Since first my spirit wandered forth
  From the drear cities of the north,
And to Italia's mountains fled.

And here I set my face towards home,
  For all my pilgrimage is done,
  Although, methinks, yon blood-red sun
Marshals the way to Holy Rome.

O Blessed Lady, who dost hold
  Upon the seven hills thy reign!
  O Mother without blot or stain,
Crowned with bright crowns of triple gold!

O Roma, Roma, at thy feet
  I lay this barren gift of song!
  For, ah! the way is steep and long
That leads unto thy sacred street.

II

And yet what joy it were for me
    To turn my feet unto the south,
    And journeying towards the Tiber mouth
To kneel again at Fiesole!

And wandering through the tangled pines
    That break the gold of Arno's stream,
    To see the purple mist and gleam
Of morning on the Apennines

By many a vineyard-hidden home,
    Orchard and olive-garden grey,
    Till from the drear Campagna's way
The seven hills bear up the dome!

III

A pilgrim from the northern seas—
    What joy for me to seek alone
    The wondrous temple and the throne
Of him who holds the awful keys!

When, bright with purple and with gold
    Come priest and holy cardinal,
    And borne above the heads of all
The gentle Shepherd of the Fold.

O joy to see before I die
    The only God-anointed king,
    And hear the silver trumpets ring
A triumph as he passes by!

Or at the brazen-pillared shrine
   Holds high the mystic sacrifice,
   And shows his God to human eyes
Beneath the veil of bread and wine.

IV

For lo, what changes time can bring!
   The cycles of revolving years
   May free my heart from all its fears,
And teach my lips a song to sing.

Before yon field of trembling gold
   Is garnered into dusty sheaves,
   Or ere the autumn's scarlet leaves
Flutter as birds adown the wold,

I may have run the glorious race,
   And caught the torch while yet aflame,
   And called upon the holy name
Of Him who now doth hide His face.

ARONA

HUMANITAD

It is full winter now: the trees are bare,
    Save where the cattle huddle from the cold
Beneath the pine, for it doth never wear
    The autumn's gaudy livery whose gold
Her jealous brother pilfers, but is true
To the green doublet; bitter is the wind, as though it blew

From Saturn's cave; a few thin wisps of hay
    Lie on the sharp black hedges, where the wain
Dragged the sweet pillage of a summer's day
    From the low meadows up the narrow lane;
Upon the half-thawed snow the bleating sheep
Press close against the hurdles, and the shivering house-dogs creep

From the shut stable to the frozen stream
    And back again disconsolate, and miss
The bawling shepherds and the noisy team;
    And overhead in circling listlessness
The cawing rooks whirl round the frosted stack,
Or crowd the dripping boughs; and in the fen the ice-pools crack

Where the gaunt bittern stalks among the reeds
    And flaps his wings, and stretches back his neck,
And hoots to see the moon; across the meads
    Limps the poor frightened hare, a little speck;
And a stray seamew with its fretful cry
Flits like a sudden drift of snow against the dull grey sky.

Full winter: and the lusty goodman brings
    His load of faggots from the chilly byre,
And stamps his feet upon the hearth, and flings
    The sappy billets on the waning fire,
And laughs to see the sudden lightening scare
His children at their play, and yet,—the spring is in the air;

Already the slim crocus stirs the snow,
    And soon yon blanchèd fields will bloom again
With nodding cowslips for some lad to mow,
    For with the first warm kisses of the rain
The winter's icy sorrow breaks to tears,
And the brown thrushes mate, and with bright eyes the rabbit peers

From the dark warren where the fir-cones lie,
    And treads one snowdrop under foot, and runs
Over the mossy knoll, and blackbirds fly
    Across our path at evening, and the suns
Stay longer with us; ah! how good to see
Grass-girdled spring in all her joy of laughing greenery

Dance through the hedges till the early rose,
    (That sweet repentance of the thorny briar!)
Burst from its sheathèd emerald and disclose
    The little quivering disk of golden fire
Which the bees know so well, for with it come
Pale boy's-love, sops-in-wine, and daffadillies all in bloom.

Then up and down the field the sower goes,
    While close behind the laughing younker scares
With shrilly whoop the black and thievish crows,
    And then the chestnut-tree its glory wears,
And on the grass the creamy blossom falls
In odorous excess, and faint half-whispered madrigals

Steal from the bluebells' nodding carillons
    Each breezy morn, and then white jessamine,
That star of its own heaven, snap-dragons
    With lolling crimson tongues, and eglantine
In dusty velvets clad usurp the bed
And woodland empery, and when the lingering rose hath shed

Red leaf by leaf its folded panoply,
    And pansies closed their purple-lidded eyes,
Chrysanthemums from gilded argosy
    Unload their gaudy scentless merchandise,
And violets getting overbold withdraw
From their shy nooks, and scarlet berries dot the leafless haw.

O happy field! and O thrice happy tree!
    Soon will your queen in daisy-flowered smock
And crown of flower-de-luce trip down the lea,
    Soon will the lazy shepherds drive their flock
Back to the pasture by the pool, and soon
Through the green leaves will float the hum of murmuring bees at noon.

Soon will the glade be bright with bellamour,
    The flower which wantons love, and those sweet nuns
Vale-lilies in their snowy vestiture
    Will tell their beaded pearls, and carnations
With mitred dusky leaves will scent the wind,
And straggling traveller's-joy each hedge with yellow stars will bind.

Dear bride of Nature and most bounteous spring,
    That canst give increase to the sweet-breath'd kine,
And to the kid its little horns, and bring
    The soft and silky blossoms to the vine,
Where is that old nepenthe which of yore
Man got from poppy root and glossy-berried mandragore!

There was a time when any common bird
    Could make me sing in unison, a time
When all the strings of boyish life were stirred
    To quick response or more melodious rhyme
By every forest idyll;—do I change?
Or rather doth some evil thing through thy fair pleasaunce range?

Nay, nay, thou art the same: 'tis I who seek
    To vex with sighs thy simple solitude,
And because fruitless tears bedew my cheek
    Would have thee weep with me in brotherhood;
Fool! shall each wronged and restless spirit dare
To taint such wine with the salt poison of own despair!

Thou art the same: 'tis I whose wretched soul
    Takes discontent to be its paramour,
And gives its kingdom to the rude control
    Of what should be its servitor,—for sure
Wisdom is somewhere, though the stormy sea
Contain it not, and the huge deep answer "'Tis not in me.'

To burn with one clear flame, to stand erect
    In natural honour, not to bend the knee
In profitless prostrations whose effect
    Is by itself condemned, what alchemy
Can teach me this? what herb Medea brewed
Will bring the unexultant peace of essence not subdued?

The minor chord which ends the harmony,
    And for its answering brother waits in vain
Sobbing for incompleted melody,
    Dies a swan's death; but I the heir of pain,
A silent Memnon with blank lidless eyes,
Wait for the light and music of those suns which never rise.

The quenched-out torch, the lonely cypress-gloom,
  The little dust stored in the narrow urn,
The gentle XAIPE of the Attic tomb,—
  Were not these better far than to return
To my old fitful restless malady,
Or spend my days within the voiceless cave of misery?

Nay! for perchance that poppy-crownèd god
  Is like the watcher by a sick man's bed
Who talks of sleep but gives it not; his rod
  Hath lost its virtue, and, when all is said,
Death is too rude, too obvious a key
To solve one single secret in a life's philosophy.

And Love! that noble madness, whose august
  And inextinguishable might can slay
The soul with honeyed drugs,—alas! I must
  From such sweet ruin play the runaway,
Although too constant memory never can
Forget the archèd splendour of those brows Olympian

Which for a little season made my youth
  So soft a swoon of exquisite indolence
That all the chiding of more prudent Truth
  Seemed the thin voice of jealousy,—O hence
Thou huntress deadlier than Artemis!
Go seek some other quarry! for of thy too perilous bliss.

My lips have drunk enough,—no more, no more,—
  Though Love himself should turn his gilded prow
Back to the troubled waters of this shore
  Where I am wrecked and stranded, even now
The chariot wheels of passion sweep too near,
Hence! Hence! I pass unto a life more barren, more austere.

More barren—ay, those arms will never lean
    Down through the trellised vines and draw my soul
In sweet reluctance through the tangled green;
    Some other head must wear that aureole,
For I am hers who loves not any man
Whose white and stainless bosom bears the sign Gorgonian.

Let Venus go and chuck her dainty page,
    And kiss his mouth, and toss his curly hair,
With net and spear and hunting equipage
    Let young Adonis to his tryst repair,
But me her fond and subtle-fashioned spell
Delights no more, though I could win her dearest citadel.

Ay, though I were that laughing shepherd boy
    Who from Mount Ida saw the little cloud
Pass over Tenedos and lofty Troy
    And knew the coming of the Queen, and bowed
In wonder at her feet, not for the sake
Of a new Helen would I bid her hand the apple take.

Then rise supreme Athena argent-limbed!
    And, if my lips be musicless, inspire
At least my life: was not thy glory hymned
    By One who gave to thee his sword and lyre
Like Æschylos at well-fought Marathon,
And died to show that Milton's England still could bear a son!

And yet I cannot tread the Portico
    And live without desire, fear and pain,
Or nurture that wise calm which long ago
    The grave Athenian master taught to men,
Self-poised, self-centred, and self-comforted,
To watch the world's vain phantasies go by with unbowed head.

Alas! that serene brow, those eloquent lips,
　　Those eyes that mirrored all eternity,
Rest in their own Colonos, an eclipse
　　Hath come on Wisdom, and Mnemosyne
Is childless; in the night which she had made
For lofty secure flight Athena's owl itself hath strayed.

Nor much with Science do I care to climb,
　　Although by strange and subtle witchery
She drew the moon from heaven: the Muse Time
　　Unrolls her gorgeous-coloured tapestry
To no less eager eyes; often indeed
In the great epic of Polymnia's scroll I love to read

How Asia sent her myriad hosts to war
　　Against a little town, and panoplied
In gilded mail with jewelled scimitar,
　　White-shielded, purple-crested, rode the Mede
Between the waving poplars and the sea
Which men call Artemisium, till he saw Thermopylæ

Its steep ravine spanned by a narrow wall,
　　And on the nearer side a little brood
Of careless lions holding festival!
　　And stood amazèd at such hardihood,
And pitched his tent upon the reedy shore,
And stayed two days to wonder, and then crept at midnight o'er

Some unfrequented height, and coming down
　　The autumn forests treacherously slew
What Sparta held most dear and was the crown
　　Of far Eurotas, and passed on, nor knew
How God had staked an evil net for him
In the small bay at Salamis,—and yet, the page grows dim,

Its cadenced Greek delights me not, I feel
    With such a goodly time too out of tune
To love it much: for like the Dial's wheel
    That from its blinded darkness strikes the noon
Yet never sees the sun, so do my eyes
Restlessly follow that which from my cheated vision flies.

O for one grand unselfish simple life
    To teach us what is Wisdom! speak ye hills
Of lone Helvellyn, for this note of strife
    Shunned your untroubled crags and crystal rills,
Where is that Spirit which living blamelessly
Yet dared to kiss the smitten mouth of his own century!

Speak ye Rydalian laurels! where is he
    Whose gentle head ye sheltered, that pure soul
Whose gracious days of uncrowned majesty
    Through lowliest conduct touched the lofty goal
Where love and duty mingle! Him at least
The most high Laws were glad of, he had sat at Wisdom's feast;

But we are Learning's changelings, know by rote
    The clarion watchword of each Grecian school
And follow none, the flawless sword which smote
    The pagan Hydra is an effete tool
Which we ourselves have blunted, what man now
Shall scale the august ancient heights and to old Reverence bow?

One such indeed I saw, but, Ichabod!
    Gone is that last dear son of Italy,
Who being man died for the sake of God,
    And whose unrisen bones sleep peacefully,
O guard him, guard him well, my Giotto's tower,
Thou marble lily of the lily town! let not the lour

Of the rude tempest vex his slumber, or
   The Arno with its tawny troubled gold
O'er-leap its marge, no mightier conqueror
   Clomb the high Capitol in the days of old
When Rome was indeed Rome, for Liberty
Walked like a bride beside him, at which sight pale Mystery

Fled shrieking to her farthest sombrest cell
   With an old man who grabbled rusty keys,
Fled shuddering, for that immemorial knell
   With which oblivion buries dynasties
Swept like a wounded eagle on the blast,
As to the holy heart of Rome the great triumvir passed.

He knew the holiest heart and heights of Rome,
   He drave the base wolf from the lion's lair,
And now lies dead by that empyreal dome
   Which overtops Valdarno hung in air
By Brunelleschi—O Melpomene
Breathe through thy melancholy pipe thy sweetest threnody!

Breathe through the tragic stops such melodies
   That Joy's self may grow jealous, and the Nine
Forget awhile their discreet emperies,
   Mourning for him who on Rome's lordliest shrine
Lit for men's lives the light of Marathon,
And bare to sun-forgotten fields the fire of the sun!

O guard him, guard him well, my Giotto's tower!
   Let some young Florentine each eventide
Bring coronals of that enchanted flower
   Which the dim woods of Vallombrosa hide,
And deck the marble tomb wherein he lies
Whose soul is as some mighty orb unseen of mortal eyes;

Some mighty orb whose cycled wanderings,
    Being tempest-driven to the farthest rim
Where Chaos meets Creation and the wings
    Of the eternal chanting Cherubim
Are pavilioned on Nothing, passed away
Into a moonless void,—and yet, though he is dust and clay,

He is not dead, the immemorial Fates
    Forbid it, and the closing shears refrain.
Lift up your heads ye everlasting gates!
    Ye argent clarions, sound a loftier strain
For the vile thing he hated lurks within
Its sombre house, alone with God and memories of sin.

Still what avails it that she sought her cave
    That murderous mother of red harlotries?
At Munich on the marble architrave
    The Grecian boys die smiling, but the seas
Which wash Ægina fret in loneliness
Not mirroring their beauty; so our lives grow colourless

For lack of our ideals, if one star
    Flame torch-like in the heavens the unjust
Swift daylight kills it, and no trump of war
    Can wake to passionate voice the silent dust
Which was Mazzini once! rich Niobe
For all her stony sorrows hath her sons; but Italy,

What Easter Day shall make her children rise,
    Who were not Gods yet suffered? what sure feet
Shall find their grave-clothes folded? what clear eyes
    Shall see them bodily? O it were meet
To roll the stone from off the sepulchre
And kiss the bleeding roses of their wounds, in love of her,

Our Italy! our mother visible!
    Most blessed among nations and most sad,
For whose dear sake the young Calabrian fell
    That day at Aspromonte and was glad
That in an age when God was bought and sold
One man could die for Liberty! but we, burnt out and cold,

See Honour smitten on the cheek and gyves
    Bind the sweet feet of Mercy: Poverty
Creeps through our sunless lanes and with sharp knives
    Cuts the warm throats of children stealthily,
And no word said:—O we are wretched men
Unworthy of our great inheritance! where is the pen

Of austere Milton? where the mighty sword
    Which slew its master righteously? the years
Have lost their ancient leader, and no word
    Breaks from the voiceless tripod on our ears:
While as a ruined mother in some spasm
Bears a base child and loathes it, so our best enthusiasm

Genders unlawful children, Anarchy
    Freedom's own Judas, the vile prodigal
Licence who steals the gold of Liberty
    And yet has nothing, Ignorance the real
One Fraticide since Cain, Envy the asp
That stings itself to anguish, Avarice whose palsied grasp

Is in its extent stiffened, moneyed Greed
    For whose dull appetite men waste away
Amid the whirr of wheels and are the seed
    Of things which slay their sower, these each day
Sees rife in England, and the gentle feet
Of Beauty tread no more the stones of each unlovely street.

What even Cromwell spared is desecrated
   By weed and worm, left to the stormy play
Of wind and beating snow, or renovated
   By more destructful hands: Time's worst decay
Will wreathe its ruins with some loveliness,
But these new Vandals can but make a rain-proof barrenness.

Where is that Art which bade the Angels sing
   Through Lincoln's lofty choir, till the air
Seems from such marble harmonies to ring
   With sweeter song than common lips can dare
To draw from actual reed? ah! where is now
The cunning hand which made the flowering hawthorn branches bow

For Southwell's arch, and carved the House of One
   Who loved the lilies of the field with all
Our dearest English flowers? the same sun
   Rises for us: the seasons natural
Weave the same tapestry of green and grey:
The unchanged hills are with us: but that Spirit hath passed away.

And yet perchance it may be better so,
   For Tyranny is an incestuous Queen,
Murder her brother is her bedfellow,
   And the Plague chambers with her: in obscene
And bloody paths her treacherous feet are set;
Better the empty desert and a soul inviolate!

For gentle brotherhood, the harmony
   Of living in the healthful air, the swift
Clean beauty of strong limbs when men are free
   And women chaste, these are the things which lift
Our souls up more than even Agnolo's
Gaunt blinded Sibyl poring o'er the scroll of human woes,

Or Titian's little maiden on the stair
   White as her own sweet lily and as tall,
Or Mona Lisa smiling through her hair,—
   Ah! somehow life is bigger after all
Than any painted angel, could we see
The God that is within us! The old Greek serenity

Which curbs the passion of that level line
   Of marble youths, who with untroubled eyes
And chastened limbs ride round Athena's shrine
   And mirror her divine economies,
And balanced symmetry of what in man
Would else wage ceaseless warfare,—this at least within the span

Between our mother's kisses and the grave
   Might so inform our lives, that we could win
Such mighty empires that from her cave
   Temptation would grow hoarse, and pallid Sin
Would walk ashamed of his adulteries,
And Passion creep from out the House of Lust with startled eyes.

To make the body and the spirit one
   With all right things, till no thing live in vain
From morn to noon, but in sweet unison
   With every pulse of flesh and throb of brain
The soul in flawless essence high enthroned,
Against all outer vain attack invincibly bastioned,

Mark with serene impartiality
   The strife of things, and yet be comforted,
Knowing that by the chain causality
   All separate existences are wed
Into one supreme whole, whose utterance
Is joy, or holier praise! ah! surely this were governance

Of Life in most august omnipresence,
    Through which the rational intellect would find
In passion its expression, and mere sense,
    Ignoble else, lend fire to the mind,
And being joined with it in harmony
More mystical than that which binds the stars planetary,

Strike from their several tones one octave chord
    Whose cadence being measureless would fly
Through all the circling spheres, then to its Lord
    Return refreshed with its new empery
And more exultant power,—this indeed
Could we but reach it were to find the last, the perfect creed.

Ah! it was easy when the world was young
    To keep one's life free and inviolate,
From our sad lips another song is rung,
    By our own hands our heads are desecrate,
Wanderers in drear exile, and dispossessed
Of what should be our own, we can but feed on wild unrest.

Somehow the grace, the bloom of things has flown,
    And of all men we are most wretched who
Must live each other's lives and not our own
    For very pity's sake and then undo
All that we lived for—it was otherwise
When soul and body seemed to blend in mystic symphonies.

But we have left those gentle haunts to pass
    With weary feet to the new Calvary,
Where we behold, as one who in a glass
    Sees his own face, self-slain Humanity,
And in the dumb reproach of that sad gaze
Learn what an awful phantom the red hand of man can raise.

O smitten mouth! O forehead crowned with thorn!
   O chalice of all common miseries!
Thou for our sakes that loved thee not hast borne
   An agony of endless centuries,
And we were vain and ignorant nor knew
That when we stabbed thy heart it was our own real hearts we slew.

Being ourselves the sowers and the seeds,
   The night that covers and the lights that fade,
The spear that pierces and the side that bleeds,
   The lips betraying and the life betrayed;
The deep hath calm: the moon hath rest: but we
Lords of the natural world are yet our own dread enemy.

Is this the end of all that primal force
   Which, in its changes being still the same,
From eyeless Chaos cleft its upward course,
   Through ravenous seas and whirling rocks and flame,
Till the suns met in heaven and began
Their cycles, and the morning stars sang, and the Word was Man!

Nay, nay, we are but crucified, and though
   The bloody sweat falls from our brows like rain
Loosen the nails—we shall come down I know,
   Staunch the red wounds—we shall be whole again,
No need have we of hyssop-laden rod,
That which is purely human, that is godlike, that is God.

LOUIS NAPOLEON

Eagle of Austerlitz! where were thy wings
   When far away upon a barbarous strand,
   In fight unequal, by an obscure hand,
Fell the last scion of thy brood of Kings!

Poor boy! thou shalt not flaunt thy cloak of red,
   Or ride in state through Paris in the van
   Of thy returning legions, but instead
Thy mother France, free and republican,

Shall on thy dead and crownless forehead place
   The better laurels of a soldier's crown,
   That not dishonoured should thy soul go down
To tell the mighty Sire of thy race

That France hath kissed the mouth of Liberty,
   And found it sweeter than his honied bees,
   And that the giant wave Democracy
Breaks on the shores where Kings lay couched at ease.

ENDYMION

———————

(FOR MUSIC)

The apple trees are hung with gold,
    And birds are loud in Arcady,
The sheep lie bleating in the fold,
The wild goat runs across the wold,
But yesterday his love he told,
    I know he will come back to me.
O rising moon! O Lady moon!
    Be you my lover's sentinel,
    You cannot choose but know him well,
For he is shod with purple shoon,
You cannot choose but know my love,
    For he a shepherd's crook doth bear,
And he is soft as any dove,
    And brown and curly is his hair.

The turtle now has ceased to call
    Upon her crimson-footed groom,
The grey wolf prowls about the stall,
The lily's singing seneschal
Sleeps in the lily-bell, and all
    The violet hills are lost in gloom.
O risen moon! O holy moon!
    Stand on the top of Helice,
    And if my own true love you see,
Ah! if you see the purple shoon,
The hazel crook, the lad's brown hair,

The goat-skin wrapped about his arm,
Tell him that I am waiting where
    The rushlight glimmers in the Farm.

The falling dew is cold and chill,
    And no bird sings in Arcady,
The little fauns have left the hill,
Even the tired daffodil
Has closed its gilded doors, and still
    My lover comes not back to me.
False moon! False moon! O waning moon!
    Where is my own true lover gone,
    Where are the lips vermilion,
The shepherd's crook, the purple shoon?
Why spread that silver pavilion,
    Why wear that veil of drifting mist?
Ah! thou hast young Endymion
    Thou hast the lips that should be kissed!

LE JARDIN

The lily's withered chalice falls
  Around its rod of dusty gold,
  And from the beech-trees on the wold
The last wood-pigeon coos and calls.

The gaudy leonine sunflower
  Hangs black and barren on its stalk,
  And down the windy garden walk
The dead leaves scatter,—hour by hour.

Pale privet-petals white as milk
  Are blown into a snowy mass:
  The roses lie upon the grass
Like little shreds of crimson silk.

LA MER

A white mist drifts across the shrouds,
   A wild moon in this wintry sky
   Gleams like an angry lion's eye
Out of a mane of tawny clouds.

The muffled steersman at the wheel
   Is but a shadow in the gloom;—
   And in the throbbing engine-room
Leap the long rods of polished steel.

The shattered storm has left its trace
   Upon this huge and heaving dome,
   For the thin threads of yellow foam
Float on the waves like ravelled lace.

LE PANNEAU

Under the rose-tree's dancing shade
   There stands a little ivory girl,
   Pulling the leaves of pink and pearl
With pale green nails of polished jade.

The red leaves fall upon the mould,
   The white leaves flutter, one by one,
   Down to a blue bowl where the sun,
Like a great dragon, writhes in gold.

The white leaves float upon the air,
   The red leaves flutter idly down,
   Some fall upon her yellow gown,
And some upon her raven hair.

She takes an amber lute and sings,
   And as she sings a silver crane
   Begins his scarlet neck to strain,
And flap his burnished metal wings.

She takes a lute of amber bright,
   And from the thicket where he lies
   Her lover, with his almond eyes,
Watches her movements in delight.

And now she gives a cry of fear,
   And tiny tears begin to start:
   A thorn has wounded with its dart
The pink-veined sea-shell of her ear.

And now she laughs a merry note:
   There has fallen a petal of the rose
   Just where the yellow satin shows
The blue-veined flower of her throat.

With pale green nails of polished jade,
   Pulling the leaves of pink and pearl,
   There stands a little ivory girl
Under the rose-tree's dancing shade.

LES BALLONS

Against these turbid turquoise skies
  The light and luminous balloons
  Dip and drift like satin moons
Drift like silken butterflies;

Reel with every windy gust,
  Rise and reel like dancing girls,
  Float like strange transparent pearls,
Fall and float like silver dust.

Now to the low leaves they cling,
  Each with coy fantastic pose,
  Each a petal of a rose
Straining at a gossamer string.

Then to the tall trees they climb,
  Like thin globes of amethyst,
  Wandering opals keeping tryst
With the rubies of the lime.

CANZONET

I have no store
Of gryphon-guarded gold;
 Now, as before,
Bare is the shepherd's fold.
 Rubies nor pearls
Have I to gem thy throat;
 Yet woodland girls
Have loved the shepherd's note.

Then pluck a reed
And bid me sing to thee,
 For I would feed
Thine ears with melody,
 Who art more fair
Than fairest fleur-de-lys,
 More sweet and rare
Than sweetest ambergris.

What dost thou fear?
Young Hyacinth is slain,
 Pan is not here,
And will not come again.
 No horned Faun
Treads down the yellow leas,
 No God at dawn
Steals through the olive trees.

Hylas is dead,
Nor will he e'er divine
Those little red
Rose-petalled lips of thine.
On the high hill
No ivory dryads play,
Silver and still
Sinks the sad autumn day.

LE JARDIN
DES TUILERIES

———————

This winter air is keen and cold,
   And keen and cold this winter sun,
   But round my chair the children run
Like little things of dancing gold.

Sometimes about the painted kiosk
   The mimic soldiers strut and stride,
   Sometimes the blue-eyed brigands hide
In the bleak tangles of the bosk.

And sometimes, while the old nurse cons
   Her book, they steal across the square,
   And launch their paper navies where
Huge Triton writhes in greenish bronze.

And now in mimic flight they flee,
   And now they rush, a boisterous band—
   And, tiny hand on tiny hand,
Climb up the black and leafless tree.

Ah! cruel tree! if I were you,
   And children climbed me, for their sake
   Though it be winter I would break
Into spring blossoms white and blue!

PAN

DOUBLE VILLANELLE

I

O goat-foot God of Arcady!
This modern world is grey and old,
And what remains to us of thee?

No more the shepherd lads in glee
Throw apples at thy wattled fold,
O goat-foot God of Arcady!

Nor through the laurels can one see
Thy soft brown limbs, thy beard of gold
And what remains to us of thee?

And dull and dead our Thames would be,
For here the winds are chill and cold,
O goat-loot God of Arcady!

Then keep the tomb of Helice,
Thine olive-woods, thy vine-clad wold,
And what remains to us of thee?

Though many an unsung elegy
Sleeps in the reeds our rivers hold,
O goat-foot God of Arcady!
Ah, what remains to us of thee?

II

Ah, leave the hills of Arcady,
Thy satyrs and their wanton play,
This modern world hath need of thee.

No nymph or Faun indeed have we,
For Faun and nymph are old and grey,
Ah, leave the hills of Arcady!

This is the land where liberty
Lit grave-browed Milton on his way,
This modern world hath need of thee!

A land of ancient chivalry
Where gentle Sidney saw the day,
Ah, leave the hills of Arcady!

This fierce sea-lion of the sea,
This England lacks some stronger lay,
This modern world hath need of thee!

Then blow some trumpet loud and free,
And give thine oaten pipe away,
Ah, leave the hills of Arcady!
This modern world hath need of thee!

IN THE FOREST

Out of the mid-wood's twilight
  Into the meadow's dawn,
Ivory limbed and brown-eyed,
  Flashes my Faun!

He skips through the copses singing,
  And his shadow dances along,
And I know not which I should follow,
  Shadow or song!

O Hunter, snare me his shadow!
  O Nightingale, catch me his strain!
Else moonstruck with music and madness
  I track him in vain!

SYMPHONY
IN YELLOW

An omnibus across the bridge
   Crawls like a yellow butterfly
   And, here and there, a passer-by
Shows like a little restless midge.

Big barges full of yellow hay
   Are moored against the shadowy wharf,
   And, like a yellow silken scarf,
The thick fog hangs along the quay.

The yellow leaves begin to fade
   And flutter from the Temple elms,
   And at my feet the pale green Thames
Lies like a rod of rippled jade.

SONNETS

HÉLAS!

───────────────

To drift with every passion till my soul
Is a stringed lute on which can winds can play,
Is it for this that I have given away
Mine ancient wisdom and austere control?
Methinks my life is a twice-written scroll
Scrawled over on some boyish holiday
With idle songs for pipe and virelay,
Which do but mar the secret of the whole.
Surely there was a time I might have trod
The sunlit heights, and from life's dissonance
Struck one clear chord to reach the ears of God:
Is that time dead? lo! with a little rod
I did but touch the honey of romance—
And must I lose a soul's inheritance?

TO MILTON

Milton! I think thy spirit hath passed away
From these white cliffs and high-embattled towers;
This gorgeous fiery-coloured world of ours
Seems fallen into ashes dull and grey,
And the age changed unto a mimic play
Wherein we waste our else too-crowded hours:
For all our pomp and pageantry and powers
We are but fit to delve the common clay,
Seeing this little isle on which we stand,
This England, this sea-lion of the sea,
By ignorant demagogues is held in fee,
Who love her not: Dear God! is this the land
Which bare a triple empire in her hand
When Cromwell spake the word Democracy!

ON THE MASSACRE
OF THE CHRISTIANS
IN BULGARIA

Christ, dost Thou live indeed? or are Thy bones
Still straitened in their rock-hewn sepulchre?
And was Thy Rising only dreamed by her
Whose love of Thee for all her sin atones?
For here the air is horrid with men's groans,
The priests who call upon Thy name are slain,
Dost Thou not hear the bitter wail of pain
From those whose children lie upon the stones?
Come down, O Son of God! incestuous gloom
Curtains the land, and through the starless night
Over Thy Cross a Crescent moon I see!
If Thou in very truth didst burst the tomb
Come down, O Son of Man! and show Thy might
Lest Mahomet be crowned instead of Thee!

HOLY WEEK
AT GENOA

I wandered through Scoglietto's far retreat,
  The oranges on each o'erhanging spray
  Burned as bright lamps of gold to shame the day;
Some startled bird with fluttering wings and fleet
Made snow of all the blossoms; at my feet
  Like silver moons the pale narcissi lay:
  And the curved waves that streaked the great green bay
Laughed i' the sun, and life seemed very sweet.
Outside the young boy-priest passed singing clear,
  'Jesus the son of Mary has been slain,
  O come and fill His sepulchre with flowers.'
Ah, God! Ah, God! those dear Hellenic hours
  Had drowned all memory of Thy bitter pain,
  The Cross, the Crown, the Soldiers and the Spear.

URBS SACRA ÆTERNA

Rome! what a scroll of History thine has been;
  In the first days thy sword republican
  Ruled the whole world for many an age's span:
Then of the peoples wert thou royal Queen,
Till in thy streets the bearded Goth was seen;
  And now upon thy walls the breezes fan
  (Ah, city crowned by God, discrowned by man!)
The hated flag of red and white and green.
When was thy glory! when in search for power
  Thine eagles flew to greet the double sun,
  And the wild nations shuddered at thy rod?
Nay, but thy glory tarried for this hour,
  When pilgrims kneel before the Holy One,
  The prisoned shepherd of the Church of God.

MONTRE MARIO

69

E TENEBRIS

Come down, O Christ, and help me! reach Thy hand,
　　For I am drowning in a stormier sea
　　Than Simon on Thy lake of Galilee:
The wine of life is spilt upon the sand,
My heart is as some famine-murdered land
　　Whence all good things have perished utterly,
　　And well I know my soul in Hell must lie
If I this night before God's throne should stand.
'He sleeps perchance, or rideth to the chase,
　　Like Baal, when his prophets howled that name
　　From morn to noon on Carmel's smitten height.'
Nay, peace, I shall behold, before the night,
　　The feet of brass, the robe more white than flame,
　　The wounded hands, the weary human face.

AT VERONA

How steep the stairs within King's houses are
   For exile-wearied feet as mine to tread,
   And O how salt and bitter is the bread
Which falls from this Hound's table,—better far
That I had died in the red ways of war,
   Or that the gate of Florence bare my head,
   Than to live thus, by all things comraded
Which seek the essence of my soul to mar.

'Curse God and die: what better hope than this?
   He hath forgotten thee in all the bliss
   Of his gold city, and eternal day'—
Nay peace: behind my prison's blinded bars
   I do possess what none can take away,
   My love and all the glory of the stars.

ON THE SALE BY
AUCTION OF
KEATS' LOVE LETTERS

These are the letters which Endymion wrote
    To one he loved in secret, and apart.
    And now the brawlers of the auction mart
Bargain and bid for each poor blotted note,
Ay! for each separate pulse of passion quote
    The merchant's price. I think they love not art
    Who break the crystal of a poet's heart
That small and sickly eyes may glare and gloat.

Is it not said that many years ago,
    In a far Eastern town, some soldiers ran
    With torches through the midnight, and began
To wrangle for mean raiment, and to throw
    Dice for the garments of a wretched man,
Not knowing the God's wonder, or His woe?

THE
NEW REMORSE

The sin was mine; I did not understand.
  So now is music prisoned in her cave,
  Save where some ebbing desultory wave
Frets with its restless whirls this meagre strand.
And in the withered hollow of this land
  Hath Summer dug herself so deep a grave,
  That hardly can the leaden willow crave
One silver blossom from keen Winter's hand.

But who is this who cometh by the shore?
(Nay, love, look up and wonder!) Who is this
  Who cometh in dyed garments from the South?
It is thy new-found Lord, and he shall kiss
  The yet unravished roses of thy mouth,
And I shall weep and worship, as before.

Made in the USA
Las Vegas, NV
24 April 2023

71045664R10049